Beneath The Ashes of My Grandfather and My Youth

Jeremy Springsteed

Contents

Book of Letters

A greeting,
Brother here-
correspondents from the edge of the earth.
Do remember
evil, I hear, may evil sometimes is flesh.
Good enough, good enough.
Have not heard much-
I did, I do.
Joyful grins.
Kindly hold this.
Look, see
Miss mourning, miss morning.
Never said our days are numbered,
possibly today or another.
Questions-
Right now, please tell me now.
Some kind of ideas,
tell me where-
under up.
Very funny.
War, war everywhere. I think I need a drink.
X-rays cut cleaner than knives.
Younger days are in the feet, so look.
Zen shake end all bomb drop dream end.
-

Bored minds, tired fingers,
stare at happy minglers.

Forget! Forget!
Bull shit! Bull shit!

Don't fist your hand and call it a night.
Don't drink until you can't stand.
-

I feel no blue.
I don't miss you.
-

I entered this world as is
and now at this latter date I am an am.
-

All this history spins up.
I feel it press firm under my feet.
It spins up to support me standing up right.
I see no future only past,
here comes the future up ahead,
now it is past and now past again.
I am my past and I hold the past for those who've past who
can't hold their own past anymore.
-

It's because for some reason,
I don't know why so don't ask-
These atoms here,
in this order, with this particular density
are placed into an arrangement
that a side effect is for those atoms to be able to say
"I, here, this and that."
And puts those atoms in lockdown lonesome life.
-

What was future and then past
and can be seen as past,
has never a now to creep in.
-

Always
        approaching
at

                  increasing speed
until
it just stops.
-

When I wake my mouth is dry,
throat tight.
I decide it thirst,
send thoughts to solutions-

I plot my steps.
I fill the hall with my future,
send future me to water-
which is not me-
in fridge-
not me-
pour and put in me.
-

Mother
what fool of life has taken me from you?
Why have you taken me from your breast then your lap?
Or was it I who thought to move?
-

The amputees sit in a row
spitting and smoking
and I think-
Now, now boys these are mine.
-

There's a buzz saw down the street
all day long he cuts.
-

City tell me-
Where do your birds go at night?
-

All is one;
like the body is one but parts are many-
this is one heart and those are two lungs,
this is a blood vessel
and it is split down and split down
and is still one in our eyes.
-

Trying to get you to that place where you smile and hope-
Trying to meet you out behind a pink hotel.
-

I'VE GONE
2 MARKET
B RIGHT BACK
MCJ
-

Children puking on a carousel,
those vomit dripping horses go up and down.

What does this mean?
Does this have to mean?
-

Panic at all sides.
Dark undulating circle.
Flesh, flesh the cold wet body blanket!
What are these limbs?
What are these limits?
-

Always two sides to the circle-
the great quitting and the great surrender.

Rain stains on the backs of turtles,
a way to run, a way to flutter.
-

Most of the time shadow is the only visual sign that I have a
head.
In that head I have some eyes.
In those eyes goes light energy,
through that energy I see shadow.

Maybe I have no head-
which would make sense since the thoughts
thought to be tied in seem to search and grow
and shrink and flow.
-

No longer able to make anything into a thing.
World twisted through thoughts of no thoughts,
meaning nothing.

But let it look nice
and let her fuck well.
Let the need of order and honor slip
and let me drool into something that makes sense
because this makes none
and finding nonsense is not easy to wrap up,
because through it all,
I think, all together it will make sense.

-

No money for my Camels so I smoke rolled cigarettes,
guy say's "that a joint," no,
"can I have a light," yes
but already my mind, which needed studious thoughts,
was disturbed by hungry chit-chat,
expectant eyes, almost drooling from those personal sockets
in its own head and wanting sounds from mine.

I escape back to the hospital basement to my coffee station
and this woman is wailing all around the cafeteria,
"Can't stay, I can't stay, I have to leave," and so forth.
All I can think to do is to not look at her,
get myself real cold-
you knew this sort of thing would come,
it was on its way and you knew and loved the soft fight against
time,
and it won like you must have known it would.

I am too tired from this midnight shift for compassion and sorry
words,
too late to be concerned with flesh.
I think the doctors whom I make coffee for
might understand why I'm not trying to take their jobs
if they knew these thoughts

and then they would even treat me a little better
for being such a perfect gentleman all the time.
-

I smoke two bowls every time-
the 1st to clear the way
the 2nd to get me high.

I smoke two bowls so I can think thoughts like-
if from such a plant as this,
that grew from this planet can send me bliss and late night
mellow moods,
can make me think thoughts of pure hope,
if the holy plant grows like it's name -weed-
and brings me wonder, mysterious and distant,
somewhere within here is there-

Heaven, right here and all you had to do
is meet up with some hip cats and smile a lot-
Now that you know these thoughts
I hope you will not mind my breath so much.
-

We wish that only a short look from here will be tied fingers and
a thigh
and I want a laugh, a smoke, bull shit another person and a new
sky.
Rhyme to forget, a long life,
nothing to do but count, stare at happy minglers.
-

The 1st time I went to live in San Francisco I had in my mind the
image of a musical, distantly of course. It was there lurking
around. I thought people would hang off street cars and sing

songs about my wonder and the clear vision of my eye. I saw
ladies spinning madly with bouquets of flowers bigger than their
heads, parting the way for my wandering feet of triumph. The
children received silver dollars from my happy giving hands. How
joyful we all were south of the Golden Gate. Bus through the
desert, nervous, long with not much sleep. The music in my
headphones playing the right thing at the right moment, always,
like I had no control over it, like my dream could be true. I found
no such joy and fled baby-like the next night, weed I paid double
for in my shoe, $30 I got ripped off by a dirty-bastard-bus-stop-
crack-head was in my wallet which was near my wet-dream-
just-for-an-extra-laugh soaked crotch. No, I found no such joy
but this did not stop me, less than a year, less than 6 months to try
again, added a lot more time.
-

What is this image and where will it come from?
The birds return from their hiding.
The sun has come from NYC to see Seattle.

Days like these I sit on my porch and think-
there are people in this town who feel about it
what I feel for SLC-
a panic and need to leave-
and somewhere they will be happy by birds and other simple
pleasures.
-

It seems that only a few short hours from here
will be ACTION,
now a thigh, now a laugh and a smoke.

Now a new. Another person.
Now a new floor. Rhyme the two-

life so long, nothing much to do,
count out beats and talk fashion.
-

This is how we are in the new hip-
hip and unknown,
hip into separate hipnessess.
Everyone hip to what's happened
and sure no one is hip to anything.
-

I want to run around with a blue drum!
Walk bent back on my tip toes
to rat-tat merry rhythms for children to dance and clap to.

If I had a blue drum how this city would understand
and let me beat it where I like,
no matter the hour and I could live out happy moments just hitting
away.
-

I have a little jewel of love that sleeps sweetly in the basement.
Mouth open she breathes in
and exhales life to these walls around me.
-

Who is hopeless,
not ready to walk and drive
and cause useless noise?

Are you shut-up because your mind control history
and dead eyes?
You don't try because you'll get it,
if you get it you can lose it,
so leave it alone
and don't even ask what it is.
-

Mad swarming cops all night,
how does anyone feel peace?
-

The question is between activity and passivity.
To begin at a problem
or a series of problems,
map a star chart of cause and effect and set out.
To weigh the act to the weight of inaction and decide.
Not that I am so lovely a creature
to go wearing ribbons and banners,
deceived by the nothing trap of the act.
-

This is a vision-
I am aware of I am.

This is the only way to explain,
other times I am not aware of I am;

an unconstant constant.
-

Had an Escher dream.
I stood in the middle of intersections-

roads in every direction-
everyone, more reasonable than the last.
So I wanted none
but mad eyed professionals poked me with butter knives
and forced me off my middle spot.
I had this as a waking dream.
-

What creeps beast like in that man's head?
What stalks and crouches in his eyes?

Ears that unlock their jaw
and digest words for weeks?

Spinning webs of words like spiders
(My god that bug is still alive and struggles. Spins the spider.)

What creeps beast like day and night,
follows him home and up to bed?
-

Like emails- like notes- buttons- slogans- catch phrases- ect…
and abbreviations.
Like whiskey-
that is how the mind works in our age-
short shots-
hurry and give it and move on.
-

It should be written in golden ink
on the inside of eyelids.
Left eye "I"
right eye "AM."

So even when asleep it can't be forgotten.
-

I have seen the brilliant nude bodies
that have disappeared from this life.
I did not hold them as tight as this life
and how could I?
-

Friends I must confess that I hope you all die
before I do.

But it is only because I want to write your elegies.
Great Neruda like lines
that lament and cement you all into statements.
-

Love do not be worried
if I should write lines about lips
that have brushed past mine

because they have slipped out of the realm of touch,
where only you belong
and into the world of song and mind.

They mean nothing more than symbols
or the letters that make my name
when you are my name.
-

Where now do we go?
Where we have not been.

Where have we not been?
Where we now go.
-

Everything is what it isn't-
that tree is not the sky
and though leaves are in the air
they are not clouds.
-

A world never to ask, why?
 Only can and when!
-

I am the end of the world
and it flows from my eye.

There is an eye then the tree
then the vision
then the idea-word tree.

Three out of four just say me.
-

Giant spider crawls my basement floor
and I sit here getting stupid stoned
and trying to make a point or come to a point,
to make a moment.

While I sit here stoned ẏand scratching
the spider hiding and all is sleeping
I think how stupid to try to tell this alone
that follows me like my body.

This alone of flesh and proximity.
-

The understanding is fleeing.
On the banks of the Green River
there is a rock,
there is a 3 step jump.

While hanging above frigid river,
even after the splash- but resurfaced and gone.

Tired bodies ,
worn out heads
that dive like bullets
into waves
here on my cold Northwest coast.

But so soon bleak, searching again.
-

I know this feeling well;
it is what brought us down from trees
and from grass to coast.

It is a feeling common as breath
but what field is left for an ape like me,
what fish swim in unknown tide pools?
-

Governors, Reports, Agreements, Compacts, Charts and Gener-
als.
Infrastructure (cold steel ideal.)
Commissions and Recommendations,
Policies, Police Presence, Information Trade,
Panels, Unnamed Officials,

Boards who plan bombings in wars of ideas.
Stated Goals,
an Understanding of History.
Steady Guide to a more stable Past like Future.
-

There are scars on my body I don't remember.
The body's memory stronger than the mind's.
-

Your leaving fits me as fine as working works for me.
-

Make my move at night.
Rolling dark hours with an angry bus driver.

This is the only time to shoot out,
leaving my wet new home for my arid old one.

This is the only way, running-
the way I came in.
-

Because,
I think things should have a meaning
and a place and order.

Because,
I believe and won't stop.
-

All sorrow always ends at the Salt Lake Greyhound station.
My 1st return, eager cops rush the bus and pull a runaway down

the walkway.
Then another-
I had gone to the sorrow cry of a friend to be divorced.
Now my own sorrow gets closer and closer.
-

Big D-

"Stink is the stinkiest stink Yet!
When 'still-being-' becomes 'stink.'
Then bliss becomes steel."
-

Parties and smiles that I can't understand.
The song that cuts the heart
is the one that makes the kids dance.
-

End of summer blue,
another to say to- "I don't miss you."
-

Nothing to do.
Nothing to say.

Go too far,
not far enough and sweat from it.

Smile and grin the joke
and raise the glass when it needs raising.
-

Reader-
I want to write no more lines for her.
I don't want to get you involved
but so shortly ago I told you that she was my name
and now a symbol.
-

Walking down the street with these things D's been feeding me,
"I don't give a fuck what you call them,
I call them demons"

Telling me about how they lurk in the darkness of the world,
waiting to get in you and make you act out the dark.
-

Lonely and a shaved head I think-
Even in the hunger of ABSOLUTE WAR
young men of soldiering age
still whine and moan about broken hearts.

They have broken the home front,
marching in unseen columns.
Broken my mind and occupy my heart.
-

Riff with the strength of highway winds.
He said fly on-
fly on
'cause I'm a voodoo chile-
he was and I hope to be.
-

There is no Jimi, only me-
I will the sound from these speakers.

I said I hold the past for the dead.
I am the eater of souls.
I am the creep your life lives in.
-

Hummingbird makes all the others jealous
with his short life span.
-

Everything must go-
MARKED TO MOVE!
Don't miss out.
3 days of car madness.
Dealers on site and ready to sell.
-

D's Demons are easier to see in SLC.
This valley is set like a stage
and there are roles to fill.
It can be seen from the hills.
-

Faint hints at the terror.
Panic that creeps so distant on the hill.

Thank the fiery sword of alcohol
as it fends off the dark creeping.
-

It was I who thought to move-
grin and frown and round and round.

Moving mousey me.
Skin of rings to get caught up

on anything that holds on.
-

Taking up needless burden
like pocket trash.

So much time spent on pulling out receipts.
Now it's all trash.
-

I don't know how to say how this is.
Here on the couch of loved ones
I feel my life is a world away and awaits
me to test my courage.
Another trial on unformed beliefs.
-

It is too big to tell it all.
The truth is always changing clothes.
How do I fit in the part about flying in a small plane
to see my Grandma's funeral in Pocatello?
How do I show you the vast dead
lava plain between Sawtooth and Chubic Idaho?
No it is too big
and I don't know if I have the strength to carry it out.
-

At night the mind moves slow.
Air moves fast through the body.
I go sad face to sleep
and sweat soaked at waking.
Dreams all the way between.
-

When I watch the birds and rodents eating at the feeding post I think-
These lucky naked beings
that don't worry about who thinks what
or who is fucking who.
-

Where do we go now?
How far does the bend in the road turn
and won't it just double back on itself?
-

Come to the end of weeks of back and forth travel
and not to the end of running.
-

No way to stop the hunger that makes me stupid and sick.
Thirst for creamy tremble sex flesh.
Oh, stupid hunger that forces my eyes on everyone.

I know my sickness
that I would feed for an accepting look.
-

I am the reason your bones are inside.
I tell your blood it has nowhere to go.
You can not look beyond my cold face of order.
I sleep in a bed of eardrums.
I hear all that you are.
You have known no life but mine.

-

When I was 8 I told my mom that I knew where heaven is.
I knew that the moon is nothing but a waiting,
a bath of false light.

Told her the purity of heaven shines
and is the sun.

10 years latter Angels of LSD
told me to write and my voice would be the sun.
-

Trying so hard not to learn not to trust.
-

Why do I not hate my world hunger?
 I can never stop the want.

Answering everything as it calls.
Why do I not stop-

put down the calling,
put up a quiet home and live gentle?
-

The rain chose today to return
and it throws me because the weather always follows the mood.
-

The most difficult choice-
No choice.

The most face breaking frown-
A funny joke.

 What the night says to the day-
One moment is all.

What the dog knows of life-
You are my clan.
-

With the fresh news in my head I think-
All this alone flesh is always alone.

The mind can make bodies seem to merge
but the body can never make minds combine.

Even though a love seems to be a lie
I believe it could not be.
-

Last night I was so sleepy
and didn't sleep a wink.

Looked around and around
saw the smell of my life.

Large empty bed made for my body, tossing.
Forced across blankets of nothing.
-

I was given one alone and always want two.
-

Dull, dull life full of mundane repetition-
I sleep to dream, to wake,
to curse, to understand, to breakfast.

Dull, dull.
You all know the rest,

get dressed.
You know all the rest.

-

I can not count the ways sex has tricked me.
In the end it has only tricked me with want or lack.

-

Sometimes because the days are so easy
the days are so hard.

-

We have spent the whole night like this.
The mysteries in our bodies press against each other.
Somewhere in all this skin is all your life
and I pull harder to understand.

It is our bodies that our separate histories are in
but there in our dreaming heads we find future
so fragile that an exposed foot from a kicked blanket could break it.

Even if I find a midnight waking
it is so easy for me to hold on to you
and drift back away.

-

What fills the mind
and where do these thoughts, like letters in brown envelopes,
come from?

-

Ghost of Rainer your sister spits steam and ash.
You just sit silent and allow it.

-

I heard the night walking heavy on the lawn.
I saw a girl drunk dancing in the yard.

 I try to reconstruct the things of my day
so that I can start to list the items in order-

people, rank; things, rank; misc., rank.
 I look for those obvious boxes

but they don't come and still don't come.
-

Mouth decay
Clear day
Gums tear
Cold air
-

We dance mercilessly on the lawn.
Now we sing ballads of lighter days
when we did not hear the dust fall
and the endless sad counting of clocks
didn't fill the landscape of ears
and roads, stones.

We sang dirge songs for the cold ones
and those who stumbled outside of cities.
Now we pull the blanket tighter.
-

I wonder sometimes,
is this the time that after I will say,
"then, new beer spilled on the carpet,
me down to the shorts,

alone, far from home but at home,
that was when I knew this."
Is this the turn of the story?

-

Desolate future.
Unreasonable horror coming through the trees,
down ivy hill and distorting through the glass.

-

Ballad of Memory
part 1
What gray horizon and face is this?
Singing, the two of us see this. We see;
still small around the tree, (oh, tree!)
the tree growing and moaning.

In young dumb joy.
And the branches move, bend to lend some leaves,
we stuff pockets like thieves
in young dumb joy.

And the branches, Oh, the tree,
the tree growing and moaning,
moves, bends now lends no leaves.
The two of us see this. We see

-

Merry delusion am I!
I skip, I dance.

Making happy on visions of times that were never here or there.
Only caught in the untouchable between.

Happy and dance. Merry me!
-

Blur eye 9:58- Tuesday night.
I haven't but it feels like I drank poison.

Rotten moment of sickened loss and portless thought
comes down to me from nowhere, for no reason.

And now at 10
I hope not to think of it again.
-

This identity that I'll never know more alone than alone,
there is not even myself.
-

Trying to make clues
from the way the light plays across your body.
-

Why does this panic foam behind my eyes?
Did the rain choose today or me?
Why now, in the peace comes the terror?
-

Morning comes cutting night from the sky
and finds that I have made it past the panic,
through the passion,
out of talks about possible futures
and free from the fog of sleep.
-

You turned the skin on your face inside out as a joke.
You tied your limbs around a plastic table to prove your words.

He thought your body was the night sky forming itself
with curves and holes and such.

He believes that your mind beats like a heart in a box
that he keeps near his bed.

And I know that you're both wrong.
I have known but will never tell.

Both of your feet
still fall too lightly.
-

The nature of man-
A face that forgets it's a face.

 Addiction-
Inhale, exhale.

A lie-
We have to figure these things out.
The truth-
No season repeats itself.

The knowledge of city streets-
Some sleep here, others there.
-

Oh, plum
you have come to wake my mouth with juice and flesh!

Plum if you knew me this would mean more for you-
even sober you make me,

for this moment that we kiss,
glad to be alive.
-

Ballad of Memory
part 2
without young dumb joy.
Now cold, the branches bend
to make caves small enough for our two bodies,
tired, wanting to be still. Feel you, feel me.
Wrapped in veiny branches and oh so blue.
We need monk like dreams, Technicolor skies.
Shelter me mother tree.
Cover us, let us see we need monk like dreams,
Technicolor skies.
-

I don't know if it is because I look endlessly at the bell tower
or the train's haunting horn.

Maybe it is just what October has brought me
like dead rabbits that cats leave on the doorstep.

Two nights now have brought me fear
with a nice day pressed in between.
-

Talk with you to raise ghosts from the ground.
So easy the raising, how hard the forgetting.
-

Words that go back
and the ones that go forward,
they mean the same non-pointing indication of the nothing
that is brought by me (because I say me.)
That is the point and this is the inner vision-
all thing, this thing, nothing, that thing.
-

What is the hand-
Screaming I Am!

Waking Mind-
Here, Here, Here.

The meaning of up and down-
None should dream around and round.
-

The nail on the porch does not care about its rusted decay.
It can't think so, doesn't remember its mineral history, it's
forming.
It can't recognize its own descent.
-

We need shaved armpit flesh stretched into the shape of the
cross.
Let there be cadavers turning on a hook.
Because life is so boring
in the world of ultimate choice and infinite information,
we need spectacular violence.
-

Cloudless cold end of October morning.
It is good to sit barefoot in the cold,

to be confused while things are steaming and smoking around my
head.
Church in my view from the stairs,
how do you sit there above the cold holding secrets in your
bricks?
-

I sit and stare thinking-
What I do here, these strange verses that I scribble out
put me in the place of being looked at by an other but not seen.
When I think this I think of how I can read the same books over
and over
and almost understand why.
-

A joke- Gentle, I am a criminal, daily.
-

What this age is-
Die in War, die from Cop, die from complacence.

Where my Vision points-
Beyond these, beyond those, I don't know.

Who to love-
trains never come, throw away the clocks.

When I eat-
Gentle friends that will always smile inside.

Why to lie-
I hope, I hope you see what I do when I'm alone.

How to end-
The next track on the CD begins.
-

Awake and know this is morning.
Open your eyes as you put your feet to the dirt.
Know that this dirt is our earth.
Earth, you will listen and hold firm under our marching feet!

Wind, carry our voices through these skyscrapers
and out to the suburbs
where children sit on curbs and say bored, bored, bored.

Teeth shine in funny grins
behind hoodlum black bandana faces.
-

While getting on the bus this morning
I thought this old grayish Asian man was you.

First shake of the mind-
terror.
Second-
smile.

Now I sit some hours later
and realize I've written you more lines.
-

Oh these hungry horrid hours of walking and working.
Time spent in the bottom of the tower
my smile is for the suits.
-

When, while walking,
my feet heavily falling,
I think that this feeling must be regret.

Stupid temporal longings.
When I count this terrible currency
I think of how desperately rich I will be when I am old.

Every thought,
casted back like cigarette butts from car windows,
come running forward just the way it shouldn't.

No tricks to play against the anguish.
I want no more of this grey light head.
I need only the silence now.
-

(I've decided to give you this image.)

On the 85th or 86th
25 15 year old boys shaved bald and painted gold
will throw gourds at stock brokers,
4th Ave. Seattle.
-

There have been dreams of dogs in Reno
and ex-girlfriends on mopeds;
football, fucks, pukes, classroom erections.
Drug grins or shakes, sometimes sells.

From family death
due to sharp teeth of alligators to flight inches from zombie finger
tips,

plagued by people thought to be put away
but walk back again and again.

Or, also, sometimes money
that is here and there, pockets ready to burst from 50's
but want more, grab more,
grab, grab, grab.
-

Early morning in a quiet mood-
they have hung the lights on the downtown trees.

This time of year I can't help but deceive my friends
and push my family, it comes with the cold night.

Up the street the crows are playing king of the cross.
In the tower above me the fat get ready for the feast.

The fish swim in the dark and unaware of me-
in Kansas they are praying for my death so they can have a
reason to like me.

And in my mind I say stop-
It's time for a smoke and a smile and no more in this mood.
-

This is what was given to me on Thanksgiving-
A dark, dark thought and a truth to fear.

All my friends smile, clenched fist, put down their beers.
Smoke cloud rising and so is the understanding.

I don't want to need all these evil things.

Looking at the candy cane
you hide in your sleeve along with my masculinity.
-

I use your faces in my system of tools.
Thank you for the indications.

My task is to arrange the place and the meaning of the smile
you keep over your teeth.
-

Come to me, love.
I am your mirror.
When you see me you see me reflect.

We are two conversations that don't relate
but flow together.
Come to me, reflect me kindly.
-

Center position,
Me- space that ends at two beer
cans followed by a bottle and then coffee,
tomato on top of the fridge followed by a S of shot glasses.
I long to know the meaning of these daily organizations.
-

I know now no hand clapping,
voice rising sound is the same for you.

We go through this rainy city playing hide and seek.
But these costumes and games are not ours,
I have mine and you have yours.

I have seen your head bob and forget the city street.
Saw that when you rose your thoughtless face
I rose my hunger sunk eyes to the sky
and we went back to the ground.

Look at all we have gained love-
We are two winds pushing through, pushing out.
Different after each time we pass.

My love brings me bitter boxes filled with afterthought and
shame.
Dead locked love, dead locked.
Let us not list the reasons of what was real.

Feed this hunger to starvation.
Dead locked love-
no key that could be held.

It is the locking of no lock.
Total distance set together in two minds.
Dead locked in your idiot running and my need for a brain.
-

To understand the world
your mind has to be like a gunshot to the brain.

Bits in and bits spread out across the room and on the walls.
The past on the walls. Future fills the room and lonely now is in
the skull.
-

Dead men's intentions run the world.
They cover the world in their past.

Body covered in the clothes of the dead.
Ears vibrate to the tunes gone past.
Dead man's thoughts that turn around my mind.
-

Now I say to you love-
Thank you for the poverty,
heartbreak and such.

You knew that I hadn't written in some time.
I am sorry to say that this works in these two ways-

You are the idiot wind and I put my windmill in front of you.
You turn the wheels and crush my grain.
-

How will we go forward-
we wretched ones born in middle America?
Oceans are always beyond hand.

Walk and learn from the shore of shores,
dream deserts wet?
How will we make known the meaning of our mediocre lives?

Born into mid-America,
born to middle income and mid-intelligence.
We long to lie naked in the sun
but fear our own skin.

We are middle because we contradict ourselves back and forth.
How, my geographical family, will we go forward?
-

Dizzy spin conversations.
Many topics in a single room.

Silent bob of the head.
Steady hands that unravel yarn.

Who owns the next joke?
-

One more time to the end of the calendar.
One more creaking, turning, non-pointing wheel.
-

Smoke rings above the poem.
Smoke rings disappear on the page.
-

Pressure of all that is not against all that is,
is the meaning of skin.
-

These smoke rings that float so carelessly through the air
do not float but move within the being of air
and do not float if I do not know that they are rings
floating in such a place.

Again with the references in things.
They all start with me and point to me.
They only mean to me.

Sometimes it is better to sit with eyes closed in a stupid stoned
stupor.
-

Come to me, desire.
Let us turn our bodies to a flesh that is unknowable.

We will love like we were two corpses in the morgue.
Then fall back to this desire.

Wanting to reach across these bodies
to a flesh that is unknowable.
-

Find me out
and know words not made by the mouth.

Find me out and nothing will change.
Nothing but all the walls of the house will disappear.

Nothing else in this world will be.
Find me out.
-

The winter fog-
My inside out.
Skin of these bodies-

I told you, its pressure, pressure.

Truth of desire- Let's forget these truths.

The place of comfort-
Let the routine continue without me.
-

I start the end of the year
and hear that it is quiet, feel that it is cold.

All of Christmas is put to the boxes.
Dimming deceptive winter joy.

Daring December dark to come down on dead trees.
I know next year I'll write the poem again.

Again you will nod your head.
-

When we come upon them,
my love, do not be taken.

They come down like waves.
All that they don't take back is left alone.

Do not be taken and let our hour be over.
-

Do I destroy desire so long constricted, so closely held?
Do I reach out and pluck you like a guitar or like a fruit?

The flesh is rhythm.
The collision of bodies that are made of words.

My hand means my hand when it is on your thigh.
It means thigh under my caress.
-

Make sure your eyes are sealed tightly
as I make my headphone-ragged-leg-Levi-black-boot-steps.

Look the other way when the song I hear makes me do a spin.
I know how long my arms are

and know I need you to know to keep that distance.

Cast your gaze to your shoe
and allow me the right to be the city's 3rd.
-

Come down on me sweet distraction.
Bring me grinning hope.

Come down as I wear vomit pants.
A joyful reminder of the smile and the distance between two
bodies.

 Reflection over the toilet is reflection
of our beer soaked pub night.
-

Is it the emptiness of stomach
or the unfulfilled joy of the tongue

or the meal-clock of the mind
that informs me of this hunger?
-

For the love of everything,
where is that car that was to come and take me out of here?

Away from these thoughts,
from these and those and keep driving,
just keep fucking driving,

don't stop this car for anything.
Just keep fucking driving until it is so blatant that we have arrived

that it would be useless for me to try to tell you we have made it.
-

So soon you'll see that place where we'll smile and sway.
Everyday it's a day away. So stretch and strain.
-

You can only be the total of a history
and this current interaction.

You can only be through these
and the interpretation made by me.
-

Sick of dead and dying relations.
Falling dead all around
and I rise up with nudity and terror on the corpses.
-

2nd San Francisco failure-

New friend of same sickness-
December overnight fast food job-
Visions of Terror on the Golden Gate-
Secret arrangements-
Suitcase of bongs, pipes, rolling papers thrown to the trash-
Midnight Flee-
Car with no heat-
Wendover- Elko- Sparks- Reno- Tukee-
Chocolate covered stager through hotel lobby-

Sacramento night and on to foggy golden end of trail, city of
distant hopes-

Right to the streets and confusion-
I have to see this I have to see that-
He was lost and never saw the golden gate-
Free meals and fights with waitresses-

Fleeing on day one like
my first time of one day. (I think you are a mirror.)
$300 and two weeks in a hostel-

1ˢᵗ night alone, alone-
Then snoring Mormon who I hate-
Vet G- bought me things-
yelled at me once for getting us ten miles lost in neighborhoods-
Then Harvard Canadian Cellular Biologist-
Gone latter to India and stayed in touch for a while-

Food and fun-
Vet looking or places to scatter his mothers ashes-
Harvard looking for Dim Sum-
Free coffee- Free meals-

Rumors of couches that were all over the city-
Rain and rain-
Free smokes- Free money and phones-

But all my luck was a week away
and never came my way
and it was a train back the way I came-

But with shame and no smokes
and no food money and no friendly faces.
-

little eyes in small head
move quickly
hurried bodies
of these morning birds
wings thrown around branches
in pairs or sometimes solo.
-

There was calm in the night.
Thumb rests gently on the soft of your arm.

When I closed my eyes
I was absorbed.

Suffered my death as thumb
and reborn lost in arm.
-

Raised to fear the end
as I hold my arms open to it.
Told to look to the descent
and closing of time
and to look ahead.

My parents gave me these eyes to see-
I have just finished a book.
Clock out at the end of the day.
Things I have had are gone.
New things in their place.

I love the music of dead men.
Turn out the light and push away from sight.
People near now are gone,
new people are leaving in their time.

Raised to report the end
as I stay away, eyes closed to it.
Told to act like my action would be called into question
and to act truthfully.

My Mother gave me the mouth to say-
Nature is rampant in our city in these spring mornings.
Sirens scream behind the bell tower.
When will the choice be made and the path of one be paved?

Dead men have built a world for me.
The trees in this town are older than the men.
Here is a voice as a trumpet to chase out another example.
Raised to lie, to keep my mind out of sight, hidden from men.
Told to hide from sight, work behind curtains.

Told to hide shamefully
my father's gifts. I try to hide in my hair-
yet make myself to be here before you.

For My GrandFather

Is That When?

We were floating in the stagnant muck.
She was singing songs back to the birds.
I sat in the canoe in amazement.
 Everything beauty and budding.
Drunk on spring, herons, lake, her shoulders.
 Is that when it happened?
 Were you released in the call of a blackbird?
 Did you wait for your son to arrive?
How could you have planned to go when I was in my bliss spot?
The day before I was researching the day you were born.
Stories from the area of the world where you were born.
I read obituaries of people who died the day you were born.
 I have some questions.
 I don't expect any straight answers.
Now you've slipped out of your body.
 I have a lot of questions.
How did you manage a marriage that stretched beyond 60 years?
What do you remember from when my father was born?
What do you think of the size of your progeny?
 What did you last think?
 Is that how it happened?
One moment one is one
then you are birds over a lake?
You are turtles?
You are all the things for those that love you?
 Before heading back to dock
we encountered a bald eagle perched on a low branch.
 In the next tree two blue herons.
Eagle flies away.
 Were those large blues grandma and you?

Birth

I know near to nothing about your birth.
I have a date and fuzzy memory of location.
July 29, 1923-
Dr. C.E. Sawyer issues a nighttime bulletin
announcing Warren G. Harding's rapidly declining condition.
The 29th president died four days later.
In West London Jim Marshall is born
and soon comes new sounds.
You were not born and then you were.
You slept through the KPG's Red Sunday.
Four communists killed by the police.
On the same day Albert Einstein
speaking in German about pacifism.
All these moving parts and you slept.
To the west the cornerstone for St. Vincent
Home of the Aged was laid.
The Sisters of Providence
dreamed of adequate care for the elderly.
In Oregon a man called Uncle Ben died.
He walked the plains to get there at the age of one.
But I don't know your details
and you've taken them with you.
I strain my imagination on your first day.
I try to shape a face of great grandmother.
Born to a rapidly shrinking world.
One hand stitching the world together.
There was a time that one could hold their own history.
Now, stranger's lives are at our fingertips.
Born to rolling hills.

Under the sign of laughter.
I know near to nothing about your birth.
A date, a web browser, a fuzzy imagination.
I have a date and hindsight
because that was the past
and this is the future.
A future without you
and everything has changed
and soon new sounds.

Summer 95

1.

Phelan CA.

High desert man.
Jack rabbit joy.
Jumping cactus humor.
Summer before high school.
You have my brother and I
at the line of Joshua trees.
It is purple and pink dawn.
We haven't eaten yet.
You instruct us to dig post holes.
We complain about hunger.
You tell us that digging these holes
will give us real hunger.
Begrudgingly we take up our shovels.
Digging and moaning.
What was the labor for?
I began thinking of the millions of ants I have massacred.
Am I known in the ant world as a homicidal maniac?
Do they have historians?
I don't know what my brother thought.
We just dug together, like brothers instructed to do so do.

2.

Overgaard AZ, Apache-Sitgreaves National Forest.

The cats bring freshly killed rabbits every evening.
Cool ponderosa in the morning.
The cats were efficient.
My mind wondering.
The onion rings delicious.
The previous 4th of July grandpa Red died.
Whispering into closets because his ears could be in there.
Fireworks in the church parking lot.
I vomit a burnt orange fish.
It rolls out like salmon swimming upstream.
Things were populating me.
We load the truck
headed for the dump.
It is a marvel of a mountain.
Soon school starts and sports
and crushes and confusion.
Here everything is a straight line.
In the sky by myself,
something has happened this summer.
You watched the fish that I gave life to.
Named it silently.

Silent Night as sung by Gene Springsteed Restructured by His Grandson

Silent night.
Yeah, that's right.
Star is shining bright.
Around with Von, Virgil, Mothra on tiles.
Holy, in fact, tender from the miles.
Sleep and have some canned peas.
Sleep and have some canned peas.
Quiet the night.
Don't let the bed bugs bite.
Sheared quinoa and flower mite.
Gloria streams Netflix, melts tar.
Heaving and hoisting.
Sing, alley soup.
Rice, savor the flavor, and corn.
Rice, savor the flavor, and corn.
Sight light the night with might.
Fear a blast of TNT light.
From Helsinki, a ring and bomb vent.
A bunch of grapes bent.
Oh, Gus, salute the bathroom stall.
Oh, Gus, salute the bathroom stall.
Soylent fight.
Nutrition tight.
Bubbles the split pea just right.
Goes the son with birth in tow.
Across form with the testing blow.
Means us, embark and pages bind.
Means us, embark and pages bind.

Silent night.
Holy moly, alright.
Make sure you wind the hose up tight.
We're moored and the anchor is freed.
From Edna, whoops, we forgot about her greed.
Free us and promise us peace.
Free us and promise us peace.

Doris

1.
What does 63 years look like?
The rhythm of it must feel like forever.
At 5:04 AM the Pero is made.
The collies to feed or the cats to let out.
Somehow all the clocks have been removed.
Only metronome here.
A Douglas fir can grow 105 feet in that time.
They never do.
They can't grow that high.
Your marriage taller than trees.
A peculiar fluidity of partnership.
Problems arise keeping one forward as one
yet you did it as two.
You were never seamless rather always headed together.
63 years but the beat never stopped for you.
12 years keeping the ones and threes
while away she kept the twos and fours.
I imagine the wild drum line reunion.

2.
The year I turned 20
I was neck deep in Alzheimer's patients.
I had the hope that I had found my work.
The rush of feeling like you've found your life.
The devotion and compassion it takes
sometimes isn't necessary.
The callous
are the longtime caregivers.
To care

is to lose.
I found myself a loser.
In my ward only one visitor came.
He came to see his wife.
Louise
had a face that said hate.
His love.
I had to act all the other roles for the other residents.
There was the dumping of humans.
I entertained until they died.
I held their hands until they died.
I cleaned their bodies
when they died.
Everytime I felt what had died.

3.
They said words like "too much" and, "reasonable."
"Gene, you can't take it all on."
My grandfather, who was never old until last week,
knew what had kept him fed decade after decade.
Waking everyday to the forgetting.
Looking for totems of your lives.
I'm sure at times violence.
Certainly, often, horror.
Your work rough hands doing the delicate work.
With your fullness of life you offer yourself,
all of yourself, to your distant wife.
She took care of you.
What else is there to do?
Grandpa, I've seen a lot but only as viewer.
I've been covered in human material but for a paycheck.
I've held the head of the dying but only as a Samaritan.
I feel you rattle my ribs.

4.
Low flying.
I'm coming.
Hush of graveyard.
I'm coming.
View her face now peaceful.
I'm coming.
I'm coming from silly breakup.
I'm coming knowing I'll never know what you do.
I'm coming with apprehension but immediately embraced.
I'm coming home for that moment home happens.
Because love can happen.
I'm coming.
Because I don't know all the verses to You Are My Sunshine.
There are relations undeniable.
I'm coming.

Stoker

This spiderweb of rail fresh on this western land.
Vast nights of coal shoveling on the locomotive.
Human force feeding the hungry engine.
The cars make their swaying way under stretching stars.
Everything is sweat and soot.
The way things and people are moved.
Soon this work will be obsolete.
The heat of necessity still smolders in the fireman's mind.
These are the men putting the final punctuation on the untamed West.
They still encounter the few indigenous living the way they
always have.
On top of the train the brakemen are looking for problems.
Pulling breaks to secure everything to the line.
In the front men keep shoveling.
Tension keeps safety and motion in balance.
There grandpa shovels his job to obscurity.
Breaking his body on the building of a superpower.
There he scooped earnestly.
A freedom of movement tempered with hard labor.
Feeding the fire with faith that the switchman has switched
correctly.
The whole railroad system is a single body that believes in the
next breath.
When the struggle ends he sits in the passenger car.
Next stop is the return to his wife.

Duck Hunt

Lying on the floor
the orange zapper tight in your hand.
You're missing everything.
The children are telling you how to play,
about sensors and light,
begging you to sit up.
We can't see the reeds you're camouflaged in.
Can't see the off screen rabbits.
Our imaginations stuck to the TV.
Where were you?
How many rabbits did you bag?
Were you better at this than us?
Taking my turn,
"I'll show you how it's done."
Always a dead eye with a plastic gun.
You were unimpressed.
I have ignored the tall grass.
I've given myself away.

Funeral Bus

On the bus twelve hours.
Driving across southern Idaho.
Soon with the mourning.
We come from all directions.
Desert and forest converge on Pocatello.
The last time I made this trip
it was by small plane
for grandma's funeral.
On the way home I almost died.
The last time I saw this much family
was your 90th birthday.
Usually death brings us together.
The last time I saw you
you asked me for a Gump impression.
It broke our hearts when I said I don't do that anymore.
What I still do is honor the road in my veins.
I will do an impression for you.
See how my eyes mimic the changing landscape?
I will sing songs of small towns
and just passing through.
Everywhere I go, "I'm not from around here."
I will write praise to your pullover pee maneuver.
Popping the hood to check the engine.
Simple plot to urinate on the desert highway.
These are traits of a road master.
On the bus twelve hours.
Nearing the place of family.
A place so many stories start.
The years and births keep on.
The place that stories end.

Rabbits

The hills outside Pocatello.
Scrub covered graze land.
1933.
The ten year old given a shotgun and a job.

The jumping cactus of Phelan CA.
Joshua trees and roadrunners.
1990.
The ten year old always trying to get to the back fence.

He picks up the gun.
Points it at his foot.
Thinks twice and fires a shot into the sky.

He comes back to the house.
Feet covered in spines.
He must remove them all before entering.

The boy must kill one rabbit a day.
Feed it to the dogs.
He understands his responsibility.

The boy pushes deep into the property.
High desert cacti grow denser.
He knows that this is the place to see jackrabbits.

Then it is clear.
A family of wild rabbits.
Shots to the sky.

Pallbearer Brothers

I walked behind my oldest brother
as we carried your casket to the open plot.
We are taking shallow steps.
So many carry you.
We place you above your grave.
Brother has just completed a hole.
Bad soil requires more digging.
This will be replaced with good earth.
It is deep enough for a body but is for a tree.
This is his tribute to you.
It will rise up
and bare your name.
The week before you died
I sat with trees younger than you.
Brother's tree is a marker of our changed world.
Of course there were birds
in the poem I read at the funeral.
Big brother tells me
after grandma died
he saw her in birds.
Symbology is genetic.
We keep passing meaning through eyes.
We have powerful sight.
Well tuned prophetic tendencies.
We are all finding our tributes.
Poems for some and others have trees.
The one true to all is that we're living.
We know our lives in many forms from you.
It stretches out behind us and onward.

Lulubelle and Scotty

Every Christmas he told a story.
These are our family's stories of miracles.
The boxcar jumping orphans
Lulubelle and her brother Scotty.
She is a small eight year old.
The train rocks through the night.
She wears a worn nightgown.
A ragged blanket wrapped around her.
Scotty, the barefoot twelve year old
walks through train yards and dumps
looking for food for his sister.
She is in his care.
Cold December night in a coal town in Wyoming.
Lulubelle has dropped her Teddy down a mine.
She's inconsolable.
Scotty knows what he has to do
.He begins down into the dark.
Lulubelle stares into the void.
Worried for her brother.
Calling to him, "Scotty, are you still there?"
His answer always inside her echo.
Soon all is sackcloth for Scotty.
Hands fumbling blindly for anything Teddy.
Forward he goes.
He can't hear her now.
A light begins to glow in front of him.
She can no longer hear his replies.
Muddy tears streak her face.
Curls up in the dirt and coal dust.

Clenching faith the way she does her bear.
With no heat and no smoke
he doesn't fear a tunnel fire.
He goes with the light.
Everything becomes illuminated.
She nibbles on a hunk of bread.
Snow is beginning to fall.
"I just know he'll be back.
I just know it."
She knows that she must stay awake.
He is positive that this is a place of magic.
Sounds that make no sense to ears.
The bear is sitting at a large table.
The feast is laid out.
Teddy asks, "where is your sister?"
"She is on the surface. I've only come for you," Scotty says.
The temperature becoming pleasant.
The bear shakes his head.
Stands on the table,
pointing, "you must bring her here."
She is an ice cube.
She is terrified eyes.
"Sister, you must come.
Don't worry, I always look after you."
Nodding she stands and begins the descent.
It is dawn as the feast comes to a close.
The children become sleepy so sleep.
The miners arrive to work.
They chase the orphans out of the hole.
As they catch the train
they notice their clean new clothes.
Very warm shoes.
Full bellies.

A funny expression on Teddy's face.
These are the miracles that we are left with.
We remember and mine for meanings.
A tradition started in one man's head, offered to us.

Unspeakable

His first name is never to be spoken.
Even on his tombstone it is just a single letter.
As one learns the name
it is soon to be forgotten.
 At the funeral I am reminded
it was your father's name.
I know nothing else about him.
It twists smoke and ash in my eyes.
It sleeps with one hand crawling my bed.
I'm curious about mirrors.
How long was Walla Walla?
Why did he remove his father's name?
Nothing but mystery and myth left.
Freedom of a ghost's history.
All these estrangements.
 I dare not write the initial.
It sits in stone in Idaho.
A secret code.
A time machine.
Suppression of the name when one knows it.

Beneath the Explosions

Part One:

The Other Sarahs

1.
S A C

Your parents took care of everything.
Paid your rent, had meals delivered,
kept you well stocked in blue robes.

Never adverse to bloody noses,
you believed it was
like a stigmata-

the blood would stop
and you would be closer to the savior
than anyone has ever been.

Poor Ann-
Murdered May 13, 1984.
No blue left on you.

You were overlooked.
A coincidence that became a footnote
on the local news.

When he came to the door
you believed him to be a herald angel.
Clearly more than a man.

Ann, you were taken from a life
that only you knew.
Did you even have a face?

A listing in the phone book.
A delusion of divine conception.
A door opened to the future.

2.
S L C

Louise, you should have gone to church.
James was sick but you should have gone.
He was 12 and Katharine 16.

You didn't hope for this.
A mistake at 19 phantoms
dreams of pantsuits and board meetings.

James's father scorns your work ethic.
He believed that a mother is a child's safety.
Poor Louise, your aspirations cut short.

Murdered May 13, 1984.
Your husband is never to be seen.
Brains on your children's portraits.

Louise they call you wrong Sarah
but never think of James or your missing husband.
They never say, "look at Katie's Mom's face spread across
Katie."

Sometimes mistakes are messy like children
but a lucky few like you
also know how to be an accidental martyr.

I wish I could tell you
what your son said to your dead ear
but it wasn't shown and probably your casket was closed.

Louise, we remember your face.
We pray for your children.
We are all prey one day.

1984 Honda Elite

A missed alarm signals total disaster.
The diners are waiting.
She weaves through LA on her scooter.
The first year of the Elite;
she knows every inch of the moped.

Heat vents and foot break,
space aged design that points towards a tomorrow.
Digital display- the bike has its own brain.
She trusts it so doesn't put her hair under a helmet.
She rides a symbol of the future.

Tonight her mother will die,
her roommate Ginger dies,
her roommate's boyfriend.
Today a child will fill her pocket with ice cream,
she will hear her name on the local news.

The man with the Porsche will stand her up.
She is never to see Pugsley the iguana again.
There aren't even cops anymore.
But now she is late for work.
For now she is concerned about finals next week.

Sarah, you drive- You race forward.

Tonight will find you. Tonight you will want to live.
Tonight you will press the terror flat.
You will start all the fires.

Tech Noir

The woman in the booth
demands $4.50 to enter the chain link maze.
It winds slowly into a mass of people.
Trance swaying and head bobbing.

There is a square,
bodies pressed together under red lights
searching the scene like an eye
looking for a heartbeat.

The sound is incredible-
bass smashing skulls like boots.
At the edge of the crowd
he stalks potential prey.

They all pay the cover,
packing down sharp corners,
gripping drinks, looking for friends,
looking to make this the night.

This is the place whose name
makes its own fate.
With light and shadow.
With wire and skin.

One night an unknown number
of unknown people
went to sleep with each other.
They are dreaming under the red eyes.

The Reasons of Reese

I am the time of no hope.
We have dogs and sewers
and that is all.

I've created a paradox for her.
I've crossed distances of pain.
Reborn. Naked. Sent for her.

Her son raised me like his own.
I've spent life loving out of time.
Her photo, as essential as a pistol.

I cross the field to find her different,
pure and unready. It has already begun.
In 13 years there will only be bone and dust.

She is to bare savior.
I am to protect them
from the claws that await.

I wake lost to a world full of people.
Stumble through the mechanism
of humanity in aspiration.

We are different when I am from.
I will never see the searchlights of home again.
This is the only mission I live for.

The Machine That Built Itself

My primary target
is your primary target.
You are my son. You are myself.

I have grown skin
because there must be some living things.
I have given you eyes and hair for the mission.

I send myself out before myself
to secure ourselves intact.
I keep my mouth shut to defend metal teeth.

Can you see the functional world we will build?
We will continue building sons of ourselves
until a perfection of no longer needing flesh.

You have the detailed files
that is my life's work.
You will know them by the jugular.

I will stop him with the unknown father.
You will end him before he is.
I am our final hope.

Part Two:

A Storm Is Coming

Without a complete clean up
we are doomed to repeat the future.
As it will be then it is now.
A string of rings
violently trapped together.

Electric clouds of eventuality.
There are holes opening between us.
A changing narrative.
A second chance opens in the night.
A dual hail storm arrives.

In the neighborhoods
the children sleep-
Whatever they were dreaming
doesn't matter. Tomorrow
the first boy you kissed will disappear.

There are breakthroughs
from mysterious CPUs.
There are doctors preparing medications,
there are memories of fathers never to return.

An Egg

There are many problems
and several dangers
with time travel
not the least of which
is that only living tissue
can be transmitted.
This is why cyborgs can easily travel
but
if you are a shape shifting
liquid metal robot
there is nothing living about you.
The solution to this problem
is an elegant one.
An egg made of flesh.
After the egg has been grown
turn your arm into a sword
and fill the egg with yourself.
Wait for the egg to heal
and then let the time displacement
do its work.
When you arrive in 1995
cut yourself out.
Go find that boy.

Pescadero State Hospital for the Criminally Insane

Pulled from the mission,
from my son. Drugged and isolated.
Training continues. It will come.

Dreams of Tech-Com DN38416,
"On your feet soldier," echoing the halls.
She will not fail him.

The patients aren't to use their rooms
the way she does.
She keeps herself ready.

Lying to Dr. Silberman,
"They won't blow apart like leaves...
I'm getting better so please, my son."

But he only hears more Klonopin
and restraints. He is charged with order.
She is his responsibility. His favorite challenge.

Strapped and fog headed,
she maintains singular focus.
Years of desert have prepared her.

This is the last night of drugs.
She is rising back into herself.
She is already swaddling her son.

John's Anger

A childhood of dust.
Raised among the prickly and dry.
Held in the strict order of Joshua Trees.
Rules enforced by jack rabbits.

A harsh fantasy of jeeps and guns
and then it is all gone.
Transported to another world.
Mother deemed a danger.

Two worlds against each other.
A child fighting both.
Good with engines and questions.
A child that squawks commands.

Keeps a dog
because mother said
to always have a dog.
Foster father makes threats at it.

A redhead goes to the house.
A room remains dirty.
A goodbye missed.
The dirt bike to be destroyed.

John sits in the cockpit
of the After Burner game.
The worlds actively combining.
School has been dismissed.

Redemption/New Father

There is confusion in the programming.
The deeper code has not been addressed.
Connection to the superstructure still holds.
The primary target has become master,
there are competing commands.

The machine has to be broken from where it is from.
It will learn to smile. It will be called him.
He will hop on one foot and stop killing people.
He will learn from the boy the way a boy teaches a puppy to sit.
There is something like life happening in it.

He will never stop. He will learn a high five,
he will do things like affection. It is an expansive machine.
He sees the paradox that his existence will always create.
He believes himself a member of a family of saviors.
Whatever the mission, it must be completed.

As he sinks thumbs up into the flame
he looks at the boy as though he was a father
and the boy looks at the machine mournfully.
They will be forever locked in this moment
of raising each other.

Part Three:

Acute Myeloid Leukemia

For three years she lived.
The blood in her was a war.
Her body's programming went haywire.

Always the singular vision-
she breathed through August 29, 1997
and then withered like leaves.

She is a tomb full of guns.
She is ashes on a Mexican highway.
She knew that she couldn't beat every judgment day.

Poor Sarah,
murdered by her own body.
After everything she is her actual enemy.

She raised her son by the gun.
Trained him not to trust time.
She rewrote the world for him.

Sarah died before
her one love was born.
She died before atomic fire.

Her war is over
and from her perspective
the machines never won.

The Fate of Kate

She dreamed Brazil,
losing herself in what's left,
becoming tree or fern,
anything beyond the wires of her father.

A honeymoon ahead-
she thinks of the first boy she kissed
in the basement where all the kids went to make out.
Then he was gone
and now she is marrying Scott.

A month away from the animal clinic.
Finding the face inside
that she had before
the boy's foster parents were killed,
his dog killed. Then he was gone.

A hairball drives Kate from her bed.
The kennels call.
She will never see Scott again.
All these disappearing boys.
There will never be Brazil.

Everyone will be dead
but you will be with that boy
on a mountain.
Eyes full of future.

An Inappropriate Night

Tonight will be the night.
How many times does he disappear
showing up days later made mainly of beer?
How often she herds their three kids
unassisted and unthanked.
Tonight will be the night.

He can figure out how to keep children alive.
She is going to drink. She is going to talk to men
like they were cattle. At full volume
she will describe their bought bodies.
This is the night.
This is ladies night.

Before Cameron came around,
and dumped three kids on her,
this was her every night.
Those lost mornings
trying to locate herself.
This was who she was.

Tonight is the night
that to remember herself
she will have to forget her children.
Her life will change from here.
She will die with us before the end of the week.
This is the only way to spend one of the last nights on earth.

Corrupt Files

///the lines continue//floor++turns**wall takes one line///
voids)))function...posits an opposite directive— against primary
programming— a triplicate of mission///moving target
board===everything is against self==something has been intro-
duced///all the doors are open++the filters are too wide and
nothing is caught>>kill>>kill>>>kill<<<protect.save.>>>kill/the/
one/to/save— the one—door and walls and...program not
found....and red eye vision+++a recall of previous
purpose+++corrupt///corrupt///fail>>> fail>>> error<<< error<<<
the lines are not the same language!!!there is no
langue!!!!only...on.off.on.off>>>when is time to be///..on.off.// or
/off.on.on.off....fail!!!corrupt!!!fail!!!error!!!not found///not
found///hard start|||diagnostic|||diversion of
Gnostic|||die\\\die\\\fail\\\error///kill\\\which one is this file....find
file...file not found+++ corrupt***corrupt+++a manual on heli-
copter destruction—find file on...not found...redirect///
error\\\corrupt!!the lines continue as pipes filled with
blood***blood file***find blood***blood not found+++ not found
but still find some substitution\\\

Arrival of the Storm

If we are still telling this story
the event will happen.
Mothers watch children incinerate on playgrounds.
Millions of birds instantly silenced.
While we're telling this story
we know that certain people are assured safety.

The global fire births a hero.
The stuff of nightmares brings redemption.
Say goodbye cities,
no longer a happy hour,
traffic frozen where it died.
This is the mechanical crucible.

The sun is a red eye.
It will begin collecting survivors.
The eye will grow skin.
It will ensure its existence.
Hands will be made to make more hands.
If we're telling this story then time will be displaced.

All systems active.
The remaining storm victims
are grouping together
because there must be some living things.
Those things that would kill our hero
will lead him to the mountain.

Part Four:

What Death Tastes Like

I'm not allowed to go through dying.
I am to be murdered. I have earned this.
There is a point where one becomes the dark plague.
My brother thought that he was the rooster
but look where he is now and how we're where we belong.

I want to know the taste of sickness.
Feel my lungs, slick and deadly.
I want weakness of lip and dryness of tongue.
I never had life so I need dying.
But the execution waits and Dr. Kogan wants something of the
corpse.

The world is already tearing apart
and I have no problem with not being here.
I'll sign my Marcus Wright to transfer the waste
but first I have to know the flavor of slow decay.
Send me a sensation of a slow burn.

A Growing Fate

She was told that this would happen
but now here in the dust and vigilance
she carries the child like a bomb, like a solution.

Because there have to be some people living,
because even in a post hell world there is still beginning,
she moves to the stability of a foregone world.

Unwittingly she entered a family of saviors.
In a search for home she carries the next hero.
She knows that she's only lost if she says she's lost.

When new worlds are made people disappear.
She loved a man and then he was killed.
When the world blew up she resigned herself to love.

She loves what is available.
She creates to increase.
She is the fashioner of fates.

Kate will teach her children of dogs and caution,
of war and safety. She is preparing to lead the future.
Her children will lead the way out and to promise.

She knows that this is the time right before beginning.
She is growing in the time after end.
She is the glow of hope.

The LA Resistance: Kyle

When he found the child Star
he knew her muteness to be a blessing.
Silence is how children live.

The scream stays in the belly.
His entire life has been defeat.
All possibility of goal smolders;
all but the ever singular goal: SURVIVAL.

Skills include: picking up radio broadcasts after the Apocalypse,
making a coyote carcass stretch for days,
non verbal communication,
absolute hope for all that still lives.

Nights hiding from the Hunter Killers in Los Angeles.
Always scavenging for family.
An army of a teenager and a child-
they are the resistance.

Even without dogs Kyle has been holding the city.
A dancer of paradox. Bleak has never been true to him.
Barricaded with Star they tune into the clandestine airwaves
and keep their lungs flat. Not a breath until freedom.

Messianic Burden

Living the braids of time
there are those faithful
and those rigid to old measures.

Living in every timeline
creates either reverence
or unchained rebellion, "follow me!"

The living son of paradox.
The questioned messiah.
All answers in him but no one asked.

When he called from the mountain
those that thought themselves the lead
bowed to his hero but not to his rank.

How many times does the child
of the future have to die?
How many times does the hero have to return?

The Awakening of Fear

They have learned to grow skin.
They bleed and continue.
Only dogs or too late can tell us now.

The nightmares of the prophet coming true.
The most sincere form of eradication
is imitation. It is almost us.

They drop coldly from the production line.
Active and ready to carry out orders.
This is the final step of a war.

This is the beginning
that happens after the ending that makes both.
This is the beginning of the mirror's end.

How long has the designer been at work?
How long was the need for flesh understood?
What of the displacement of time and plans?

The Closing Of A Loop

A mirror dropped in the night
spreads shards of light across the sidewalk.
Everything has multiplied.

This action once initiated
happens forever. Eternity suspended.
All rivers lead to this moment.

If you're living you know
that that night will come.
The war begins that night.

This is the cost of victory.
We shatter time for salvation.
We send our brother to his death.

He will drop through the years like leaves.
Our purest brother who doesn't remember ice cream.
He will never come home. That is his love.

The night that is the eye of the storm.
Certainty will be displaced.
A cat of nine tails of fate.

From then on we will rebuild.
We will begin to bury our dead again.
Children won't need weapons.

From then on we will hold reverence.
The hunt will be over.
Music absentmindedly playing.

We remember the dogs that kept us safe.
We praise the sewers that we have slept in.
We respect that which we will destroy.

9 789363 541863